CHANTS

PAT MORA

Arte Público Press
Houston, Texas

Acknowledgements

The following poems first appeared in the publications here noted: "Leyenda" in *Puerto del Sol*; "Discovered" in *New Worlds Unlimited: Images of the Mystic Truth*; "Unrefined" in *New America: Women Artists and Writers of the Southwest*; "Illegal Alien" and "Curandera" in *Hispanics in the United States: An Anthology of Creative Literature*; "Bribe" in *The Pawn Review*; "Mexican Maid" in *Spectrum*; "Cool Love," "Chuparrosa: Hummingbird" and "Sola" in *Revista Chicano-Riqueña*.

This project is made possible through grants from the Texas Commission on the Arts and the National Endowment for the Arts, a Federal Agency.

Arte Público Press
University of Houston
Houston, Texas 77204-2090

First Printing, 1984
Second Printing, 1985
Second Edition, 1994

Library of Congress Catalog No. 83-070677,
ISBN 0-934770-24-7

For my children
Bill, Libby and Cissy
whose love and laughter
warm my life

Contents

CHANTS

Bribe

I hear Indian women
       chanting, chanting
I see them long ago bribing
the desert with turquoise threads,
in the silent morning coolness,
kneeling, digging, burying
their offering in the Land
       chanting, changing
              Guide my hands, Mother,
              to weave singing birds
              flowers rocking in the wind, to trap
              them on my cloth with a web of thin threads.

Secretly I scratch a hole in the desert
by my home, I bury a ballpoint pen
and lined yellow paper. Like the Indians
I ask the Land to smile on me, to croon
softly, to help me catch her music with words.

Unrefined

The desert is no lady.
She screams at the spring sky,
dances with her skirts high,
kicks sand, flings tumbleweeds,
digs her nails into all flesh.
Her unveiled lust fascinates the sun.

PAT MORA

Mexican Maid

Would the moon help?

The sun did,
changed the *señora's* white skin
to red, then copper.
      "I'm going to take a sun
        bath, Marta, sun   bath, *sí*?"
Marta would smile, nod,
look at her own dark skin
                     and wish
that she could lie
outside at night
bathed by moonlight,
lie with her eyes closed
like the *señora* wake to a new skin
that would glisten white
when she stepped off the dusty bus
at the entrance to her village.

Mi Madre

I say feed me.
She serves red prickly pear on a spiked cactus.

I say tease me.
She sprinkles raindrops in my face.

I say frighten me.
She shouts thunder, flashes lightening.

I say comfort me.
She invites me to lay on her firm body.

I say heal me.
She gives me *manzanilla, orégano, dormilón*.

I say caress me.
She strokes my skin with her warm breath.

I say make me beautiful.
She offers turquoise for my fingers, a pink blossom
    for my hair.

I say sing to me.
She chants lonely women's songs.

PAT MORA

I say teach me.
She endures: glaring heat
                 numbing cold
                 frightening dryness.

She: the desert
She: strong mother.

Lesson I

The desert is powerless
when thunder shakes the hot air
and unfamiliar raindrops slide
on rocks, sand, *mesquite*,
when unfamiliar raindrops overwhelm
her, distort her face.
But after the storm, she breathes deeply,
caressed by a fresh sweet calm.
My Mother smiles rainbows.

When I feel shaken, powerless
to stop my bruising sadness,
I hear My Mother whisper

Mi'ja

don't fear your hot tears
cry away the storm, then listen, listen.

PAT MORA

Lesson 2

Small, white fairies dance
on the *Rio Grande*. Usually they swim
deep through their days and nights
hiding from our eyes, but when the white
sun pulls them up, up
they leap about, tiny shimmering stars.

The desert says: feel the sun
luring you from your dark, sad waters,
burst through the surface

dance

Poinsettia

You grew green and ignored
wild in the rocky hills of Mexico
a common weed.
A brown-eyed boy
with no Christmas gift for the Virgin
picked you
though he wanted to blaze her shrine
with gold or silver or stars.
He carried you inside a dark adobe church
set you before a flickering candle
cried in shame at his poor offering.

That tear
stained your green leaves red.

PAT MORA

Discovered

She feared his eyes.
She feared the priest would know
that under the stars, while the village slept,
her young lover unbuttoned her dress
and warmed her blood.

She feared his eyes.
She feared the priest would shake his head
and say, "No white wedding dress."
And her mother's eyes would close.
And her father's eyes would burn.
And her lover's eyes would unbutton
her dress again.

Leyenda

They say there was magic at Tula.
Seeds burst overnight.
Plants danced out of the ground.
By dawn, green leaves swayed.

At Tula the Toltecs
picked giant ears of corn.
Mounds of soft cornsilk
became mattresses and pillows
for small, sleepy heads.

They say at Tula the Toltecs
picked green cotton, red cotton.
In fields that were ribbons of color.
Indians harvested rainbows.

They built palaces of jade, turquoise,
gold. They made a castle
of gleaming quetzal plumage,
and when the wind blew
small green and red feathers
landed on Indian heads.

PAT MORA

Dream

Village women say orange blossoms melt
on an unclean bride.

Today I wake slowly, scratching my scalp.
        I scratched you last night on that warm
        desert sand.

I wake feeling wax under my fingernails.
        Those nails stroked your lips, your frightening
        lips, dug into your back.

I wake wondering how to shampoo my black hair,
matted white, smelling sweet.
        You rubbed moonlight through that hair
        last night; you rubbed moonlight through me.

I wake blushing, a wax-capped bride.
        By day I laugh at our Mexican superstitions.
        At night they grab me. Draw blood. Like you.
I wake, fully wake. Smile.

Today is my wedding day, I kiss
the flowers for my hair and whisper,
"Don't tell, don't tell, don't tell."

Bruja: Witch

I wait for the owl.
I wait for Tuesday and Thursday nights
to leave my slow body, to fly.

Beneath white moonlight
I lie on the hard desert.
I close my eyes, slow my heart,
pull my life in, breathe it out
into the owl's warm feathers.

I stretch into the long free wings,
feel the air gently hold me.
Gliding above my adobe home I see
my wrinkled, gray-haired body
still, far below.

The owl and I are one.
With large gold eyes
I spy my victims. Through a dirty
window I see two nude bodies trying
to escape into each other.

I laugh and call from a nearby tree,
"Amigo, who is that woman?
Not your wife, eh? You don't taste
your wife like that. Let us see.
Our whole village wants to watch."
I laugh again.

PAT MORA

Then I fly into the night.
My work is done. A frightened husband
will run to the wife who paid me
three American dollars.

I am free
until the rooster's song plunges me
down into my tired bones.
I tilt and dip and soar.
I smell mesquite. Beneath white
stars, I dance.

New Wife

She hides all day in loose clothes,
black hair braided neatly, eyes down,
smiles quick, she glances
at her mother-in-law.

At night she frees her hair.

    "Does she know?
    Does she know what we do in here?"
Her young husband smiles,
touches her mouth.

    "No," she says,
but she lies on the pillow,
looks through his eyes,
bites on the finger he puts between her lips.

PAT MORA

Cool Love

If we were Indians, in late September
we'd gather Chamisa blossoms in the desert.
We'd cover them with river water, boil
them to make a natural dye. Sun-pool.
We'd cook aspen bark, mistletoe, small berries.
We'd remove each other's clothes gently
dip our fingertips into the pots
of warm liquid. We'd stain each other,
stroke slowly, press yellow, brown, green,
red into each other's bones and veins.
We'd brand with hot love.

But we keep our hands clean, touch
yet leave no mark.
We fear claiming what we may
not want to keep.

Plot

I won't let him hit her. I won't
let him bruise her soft skin, her dark
brown eyes. I'll beg her to use the ring
snapped from a Coke can. That's my wedding
gift for my daughter.

My body betrayed me years ago, failed
to yield that drop of blood: proof
of virginity in this village of Mexican fools.
My groom shoved me off the white sheet
at dawn, spat insults. Had he planned to wave
the red stain at his drunken friends?
My in-laws' faces sneered *whore* and my neighbors
snickered at my beatings through the years.

I'll arm my daughter with a ring.
She'll slip it under her wedding mattress.
When he sleeps, she'll slit her finger
smear the sheet. She must use the ring.
I don't want to split his throat.

PAT MORA

Love Ritual

In Mexico the dead are lured
back for a day with marigolds and
candles. Women cook rich, spicy
mole. On graves they put cigarettes
and tequila, *pan dulce*, ripe mangoes.
"Come back," they're saying, "Come
back and savor earth's sweet wines."

Outside my door I'll sprinkle yellow
flower petals. Carefully I'll place
my picture, the poem I wrote you,
a sketch of two lovers removing
each other's clothes. I'll light
green votives, and you'll be pulled
back too. And maybe stay.

Puesta del Sol

for my father

The gray-haired woman wiped her hands on her apron,
lightly touched the warm wood counters of her kitchen
as cars sped on the dirt road outside her window,
cars of young men hot for Saturday night,
beer and laughter.

The woman pushed open her front screen door,
leisurely looked at the pink summer clouds,
slowly watered the plants growing in large tin cans,
said to her small granddaughter, "*Mi 'jita*,
such a sweet time of day, bird songs, wind songs."

The *abuelita* smiled when in the last tin can
she found a geranium in bloom wine bloom,
her wine on a Saturday night.

PAT MORA

Arboles de Maíz

She smiled in the dark
when the sweet desert wind whirled
around her skin like Juan's words
spinning whispered pictures
of their first *milpa*, of the seedlings
which he daily hoed and watered
whispering to the fragile plants, "Drink
the sun for he can make you strong. Stretch
to tickle those white clouds,"
and she'd laugh at his words
as she laughed when the breeze
brushed her arms as Juan continued
with his dreams, with his magic
whispering to the *elote*, "Don't fear
the thunder, lightening, rain. Grow.
Dream of being trees, *árboles de maíz*,
a fresh, green desert forest
where I can bring my love
to walk barefoot in the cool shade,"
and she would drift to sleep smiling,
seeing cornstalks taller than saguaros
or even the agave in bloom.

Moctezuma II

Slit chests bored him.
Hot hearts and the hot smell
of blood made him frown,
until he saw the slit
on his gardeners' ears, saw the plants
      cacao, orchids, magnolia
with new, soft leaves growing
as he had ordered, changing Huaxtepec
to a garden with the blood that touched
      soil, roots, leaves,
and Moctezuma began to smile often
at the blood-smell near the pyramid
for it reminded him of his garden,
of his flowers bigger than his hands,
bigger than the hearts beating
in the large bowl where *he* now saw
red blooms pulsing, pulsing

PAT MORA

Mayan Warning

the legend of Ixtabai

Stay away from that tree.
Late at night she floats free
       hear her cry, hear her cry
all alone in the leaves that will stroke
your warm cheek, then your arms,
wrap around and around, hug you
tight will Ixtabai whisper, "Stay.
Let me touch. I've empty arms, empty
arms. Oh, I cried late at night,
hugged this large Ceiba tree, crooned
to the moon, 'Send him back to my arms,'
but I knew he was dead, and the tree
stretched its arms, dried my tears,
held me tight, and it squeezed
       and it squeezed
till its love drew me in
to the bark and the leaves
as I'll squeeze you tonight."

Curandera

They think she lives alone
on the edge of town in a two-room house
where she moved when her husband died
at thirty-five of a gunshot wound
in the bed of another woman. The *curandera*
and house have aged together to the rhythm
of the desert.

She wakes early, lights candles before
her sacred statues, brews tea of *yerbabuena*.
She moves down her porch steps, rubs
cool morning sand into her hands, into her arms.
Like a large black bird, she feeds on
the desert, gathering herbs for her basket.

Her days are slow, days of grinding
dried snake into powder, of crushing
wild bees to mix with white wine.
And the townspeople come, hoping
to be touched by her ointments,
her hands, her prayers, her eyes.
She listens to their stories, and she listens
to the desert, always to the desert.

By sunset she is tired. The wind
strokes the strands of long gray hair,
the smell of drying plants drifts
into her blood, the sun seeps
into her bones. She dozes
on her back porch. Rocking, rocking.

At night she cooks chopped cactus
and brews more tea. She brushes a layer
of sand from her bed, sand which covers
the table, stove, floor. She blows
the statues clean, the candles out.
Before sleeping, she listens to the message
of the owl and the *coyote*. She closes her eyes
and breathes with the mice and snakes
and wind.

Graduation Morning
for Anthony

She called him *Lucero*, morning star,
snared him with sweet coffee, pennies.
Mexican milk candy, brown bony hugs.

Through the years she'd cross the Rio
Grande to clean his mother's home. "*Lucero,
mi lucero*," she'd cry, when she'd see him
running toward her in the morning,
when she pulled stubborn cactus thorns
from his small hands, when she found him
hiding in the creosote.

Though she's small and thin,
black sweater, black scarf,
the boy in the white graduation robe
easily finds her at the back of the cathedral,
finds her amid the swirl of sparkling clothes,
finds her eyes.

Tears slide down her wrinkled cheeks.
Her eyes, *luceros*, stroke his face.

PAT MORA

Aztec Princess

Her mother would say, "Look in
the home for happiness. Why do you stare out
often with such longing?" One day,
almost in desperation, her mother said,
"Here. See here. We buried your umbilical
cord here, in the house, a sign that you,
our girl-child, would nest inside."

That night the young woman quietly dug
for some trace of the shriveled woman-to-woman
skin. But all she found was earth, rich earth,
which she carefully scooped into an earthen jar
and carried outside to the moonlight
whispering, "Breathe."

Petals

have calloused her hands,
brightly-colored crepe paper: turquoise,
yellow, magenta, which she shapes
into large blooms for bargain-hunting tourists
who see her flowers, her puppets, her baskets,
but not her—small, gray-haired woman
wearing a white apron, who hides behind
blossoms in her stall at the market,
who sits and remembers collecting wildflowers
as a girl, climbing rocky Mexican hills
to fill a straw hat with soft blooms
which she'd stroke gently, over and over again
with her smooth fingertips.

PAT MORA

Chuparrosa: Hummingbird

I buy magic meat
of a *chuparrosa* from a toothless witch
who catches it as it sips flower-wine.
She fills her palms with blooms,
and the bird dives into perfumed petals for the last time.
The witch claps her hands hard
and blossoms float away,
but the small body is still,
as the *bruja* plucks the ruby and emerald feathers:
soft pillow for her grandchild's head.
She dries the meat, magic meat,
which I buy to sprinkle in your wine
so you will see me, only me.
And you do.
You hover.
Your eyes never wander.
More and more
on hot afternoons
I sleep
to escape your gaze.

1910

In Mexico they bowed
   their heads when she passed.
     Timid villagers stepped aside
      for the Judge's mother, Doña Luz,
who wore her black shawl, black
   gloves whenever she left her home —
     at the church, the *mercado*, and the *plaza*
      in the cool evenings when she strolled
       barely touching her son's wrist
       with her fingertips,
who wore her black shaw, black
   gloves in the carriage that took her
     and her family to Juárez, border town, away
      from Villa laughing at their terror when
       he rode through the village shouting
       spitting dust,
who wore her black shaw, black
   gloves when she crossed the Rio Grande to
     El Paso, her back straight, chin high,
      never watching her feet,
who wore her black shaw, black
   gloves into Upton's Five-and-Dime,
     who walked out,back straight, lips quivering,
      and slowly removed her shawl and gloves,
       placed them on the sidewalk with the other
       shawls and shopping bags
        "You Mexicans can't hide
        things from me," Upton would say.
        "Thieves. All thieves.
        Let me see those hands."

PAT MORA

who wore her black shaw, black
   gloves the day she walked, chin high,
      never watching her feet, on the black
         beams and boards, still smoking,
            that had been Upton's Five-and-Dime.

Village Therapy

Sly grandmother waits until the family leaves,
peeks out the front door of her adobe home,
sees her children and grandchildren walking toward
their plot of land, another day of weeding.
Waiting is her game, waiting to fill the house
for the day with soft, cheerful companions,
baby chicks — *pollitos* — who peck the dirt floor
at her feet, peck the rice and corn she hides
for them, peck as she laments granddaughters who
were jeans, who drink beer, who kiss men on the lips
in public. She grumbles, "*¡Ay, qué muchachas!*"
as she washes the dishes, as she waters her plants,
"*¡Ay, qué muchachas!*" as she cooks beans,
as she pats *tortillas*. In the late afternoon,
this mother hen with the long, gray braid
gathers her brood, patient listeners, sweeps them out.

In the evening, when the family argues,
when her granddaughters sigh, "*¡Ah, Mamá!*"
at requests for loose clothes, high collars,
shy bodies; *Abuelita* dozes, too tired
from her day of talking to say more.

PAT MORA

Abuelita Magic

The new mother cries with her baby
in the still desert night,
sits on the dirt floor of the two-room house,
rocks the angry bundle
tears sliding down her face.

The *abuelita* wakes, shakes her head,
finds a dried red chile,
slowly shakes the wrinkled pod
so the seeds rattle

                                    ts . ss, ts . ss.
The *abuelita*
                                    ts . ss, ts . ss.
gray-haired shaman
                                    ts . ss, ts . ss.
cures her two children
                                    ts . ss
with sleep

Corrida

Being the son of a proud man is bitter,
bitter like Francisco's vomit
behind the bull-ring. The afternoon sun
spun and he heard the shouts of the crowd,
    ¡VIVA FRANCISCO!
when in a foolish moment he'd run into the ring
to fight the last bull, the bull for novices.
    ¡VIVA FRANCISCO!
And he'd panicked. The son of the proud
schoolmaster, Don Mariano, had stiffened
when the bull plunged toward him. His father
jerked him to safety, but hissed, "My friend,
bullfight or see what happens." And Don Mariano
shoved two white *banderillas* into Francisco's
wet hands. His puppet arms went up and he stopped
breathing. He saw himself run toward the bull,
    ¡VIVA FRANCISCO!
felt the animal's heat when he jabbed
the shafts into soft muscle
    ¡VIVA FRANCISCO!
felt the black blood spurt on his palms,
    ¡VIVA FRANCISCO!
felt himself start breathing again
when he ran — *corrió* — to be alone
to vomit alone.

PAT MORA

Family Ties

for Teresa McKenna

Though I shop for designer jeans,
uniforms make me smile.
Chalk-white uniforms in store windows remind
me of my grandmother who refused to learn English,
who would laugh with the women from the canneries
when they filled her small home with the smell of fish,
for the white garments piled in pale pink
boxes throughout the house.

My grandmother preferred to shop in grocery stores,
preferred buying garlic, onion, chile, beans,
to buying me gifts of frilly blouses and barrettes,
hers a life of cooking, cleaning, selling.
But when I shyly showed my *abuelita*
my good report card or recited the Pledge of Allegiance,
my grandmother would smile and hand me a uniform,
never the right size, but a gift,
which I would add to the white stack
at the bottom of my closet.

En la Sangre

La niña con ojos cafés
y el abuelito con pelo blanco
bailan en la tarde silenciosa.
Castañetean los dedos
a un ritmo oído solamente
por los que aman.

In the Blood

The brown-eyed child
and the white-haired grandfather
dance in the silent afternoon.
They snap their fingers
to a rhythm only those
who love can hear.

PAT MORA

Spring Tonic

He had been her winter secret.
Her eyes had watched
how he folded his arms across his chest
at church,
how he wiped the sweat from his neck
in the cornfields,
how he drank beer slowly
at the village *fiestas*.
Tonight he had danced with her,
no words, but his arm around
her waist, pulling her,
and again when he walked her home,
pulling her, to kiss his lips.
When she entered her dark kitchen,
she lit a candle and saw
pink, yellow, white spring flowers
floating in a jar of cool water.
She poured some of her mother's
sweet-scented tonic into a clay mug,
sipped it slowly
listening to her blood sing.

Loss of Control

For me it was an adventure
riding in a basket strapped
to a plodding burro that slowly
climbed the steep dirt road
to the mountain village
where my mother slowly entered
the rented home, saw the shabby
furniture, felt the dirt beneath
her carefully polished shoes,
heard scratching, scratching
in the kitchen cabinets,
walked quickly to another room hoping
to find a clean, sweet bed on which to lie
before her daughters saw
how pale she felt, screamed in despair
for at the center of the quilt
slept a coiled snake.

PAT MORA

Illegal Alien

Socorro, you free me
to sit in my yellow kitchen
waiting for a poem
while you scrub and iron.

Today you stand before me
holding a cleanser and sponge
and say you can't sleep at night.
"My husband's fury is a fire.
His fist can burn.
We don't fight with words
on that side of the Rio Grande."

Your eyes fill. I want
to comfort you, but my arms
feel heavy, unaccustomed
to healing grown-up bodies.

I offer foolish questions
when I should hug you hard,
when I should dry your eyes, my sister,
sister because we are both women,
both married, both warmed
by Mexican blood.

It is not cool words you need
but soothing hands.
My plastic band-aid doesn't fit
your hurt.
I am the alien here.

Pushing 100

I'm eating ugly today, she says
as peas roll off her plate
when she struggles to cut her fried ham.

You're ninety-four, I say.
For the first time I take her knife
and fork and quickly cut her meat,
embarrassed at my agility.
We have reversed roles.
Once she sat patiently and watched me eat,
ordered for me. Spinster aunt, mothering.

Why do I stutter now, she asks
mouth quivering like a baby bird's.
I didn't used to. Now the words just don't
come out. Not in English. Not in Spanish.
It's because I don't practice anymore.
In my room alone, I don't talk.

You're ninety-four, I say
and she laughs, almost embarrassed
at her age.
When will I walk better, she asks
maybe I need vitamins.

You're ninety-four, I say.
Most people your age don't walk at all.
Most people don't live to be your age.

PAT MORA

True, she says, and we walk slowly
away from Denny's, her favorite restaurant.
She's smiling, still savoring
the vegetable soup, peas, mashed potatoes
with gravy, ham, garlic bread,
chocolate Bavarian mint pie, two cups
of hot coffee.

C
r
road
s
s   Come to me.
           Break the spell.

If his eyes make you itch,
but not burn,
If his words buzz like flies
round your head,
If his hands slow your breath,
slow your blood

Come to me.
Break the spell.

I will tell:
find two roads
mark the spot where they cross,
cross two pins on the spot,
garlic add,

Paint your mouth,
tip your head,
lock his eyes with your eyes,
lead him there
to the spot,
have him cross
over the cross
unaware
of the charm

Broken spell.

PAT MORA

For Georgia O'Keeffe

I want

to walk
with you
on my Texas desert,
to stand near
you straight
as a Spanish Dagger,
to see your fingers
pick a bone bouquet
touching life
where I touch death,
to hold a warm, white
pelvis up
to the glaring sun
and see
your red-blue world
to feel you touch
my eyes
as you touch canvas

to unfold
giant blooms.

Sola

I wanted to dance through life
with a tall-dark-handsome
who would choose me, $_s$pi$_n$
me, lead me past envying eyes
while I strain to match his steps,
my hands holding him.

At forty I dream of g l i d i n g

        alone

on ice, to music no one else has heard

        arms free

PAT MORA

Mielvirgen

In the slow afternoon heat she sits
in the shade watching the bees,
remembering sweet evenings
of dipping her fingers into warm
honey, smoothing it on his lips,
licking it slowly with her tongue,
hearing him laugh
       then breathe harder
slowly unbuttoning her
blouse, rubbing his
tongue on her sweet skin,
       lips, honey, breasts
buzzing
like the bees she hears now,
her eyes closed, her tongue sliding
on her lips, remembering, remembering

Limpieza

Uno, dos, tres,
she'd count silently
to thirty each night
slowing reaching for the broom
after he closed her
door and walked away,

vientiocho, veintinueve, treinta,
waiting for him to round the corner
leaving her and her two rooms alone,
free of his clothes, his words, his hands,
and she'd open her front door,
sweep the dirt floor, push the broom handle
hard, push the dirt out, sweep again and again
till her arms ached.

PAT MORA

Mayan Heat

She had often dreamed of snow,
never seen it in the *Yucatán*
but in her sleep rubbed the cold
white on her arms,
tasted it on her tongue, cold
like *helado de vainilla*
                white   cold
When he gently pulled her
up the steps of the pyramid gleaming
in the moonlight and showed her
the shimmer of the waves, the floating
stars and moon down below,
white was still
cold, until she lay on her back,
gazed up at him, and the ice fires
in the sky burned her skin.

Letting Go

At first the cages frightened her.
She had seen them in his room,
had known he loved the birds
by the way his voice grew soft
when he described their color, their songs,
forty fluttering creatures,
canaries, finches, parrots, cardinals,
stolen by this gentle young man who
longed to feed them, talk to them,
listen to them in the still desert nights
when his *abuelita* dozed in the kitchen
and he shut his bedroom door slowly
opened the cages and let his companions
freely fly about the room where tonight
she would lie beneath him for the first time
watching whirls of red, green, gold
whirring above her,
their wildness, his wildness pressing
her, pressing her into the sheets,
frightening her yet tempting her
to join their frenzy.

PAT MORA

Juan

Their superstitions branded him.
Even when he was a young boy
marching up and down, up and down
the New Mexico hills followed by a black
menagerie — black lamb, black dog,
black cat, black rabbit, *embrujado*
neighbors whispered to one another,
bewitched, a devil's child,
dark skin, dark hair, dark companions
who even slept in his bed at night.
The boy would stroke the thick fur
softly, softly as he stroked the leaves
of ailing plants which neighbors
secretly brought to him
hoping his magic would heal them.
Often the boy peered at his face
in a nearby lake, and his tears
rippled the smooth surface of the water.

Elena

My Spanish isn't enough.
I remember how I'd smile
listening to my little ones,
understanding every word they'd say,
their jokes, their songs, their plots.
      Vamos a pedirle dulces a mamá. Vamos.
But that was in Mexico.
Now my children go to American high schools.
They speak English. At night they sit around
the kitchen table, laugh with one another.
I stand by the stove and feel dumb, alone.
I bought a book to learn English.
My husband frowned, drank more beer.
My oldest said, "*Mamá*, he doesn't want you
to be smarter than he is." I'm forty,
embarrassed at mispronouncing words,
embarrassed at the laughter of my children,
the grocer, the mailman. Sometimes I take
my English book and lock myself in the bathroom,
say the thick words softly,
for if I stop trying, I will be deaf
when my children need my help.

                                           PAT MORA

Bailando

I will remember you dancing,
spinning round and round
a young girl in Mexico,
your long, black hair free in the wind,
spinning round and round
a young woman at village dances
your long, blue dress swaying
to the beat of *La Varsoviana*,
smiling into the eyes of your partners,
years later smiling into my eyes
when I'd reach up to dance with you,
my dear aunt, who years later
danced with my children,
you, white-haired but still young
more beautiful than the orchid
pinned on your shoulder,
tottering now when you walk
but saying to me, "*Estoy bailando*,"
and laughing.

Legal Alien

Bi-lingual, Bi-cultural,
able to slip from "How's life?"
to "*Me'stan volviendo loca,*"
able to sit in a paneled office
drafting memos in smooth English,
able to order in fluent Spanish
at a Mexican restaurant,
American but hyphenated,
viewed by Anglos as perhaps exotic,
perhaps inferior, definitely different,
viewed by Mexicans as alien,
(their eyes say, "You may speak
Spanish but you're not like me")
an American to Mexicans
a Mexican to Americans
a handy token
sliding back and forth
between the fringes of both worlds
by smiling
by masking the discomfort
of being pre-judged
Bi-laterally.

PAT MORA